H A

The Merry Little Peasant
Study Guide

By Judy Wilcox

Zeezok
publishing
Elyria, OH

Joseph Haydn
The Merry Little Peasant
Study Guide

ISBN 1-933573-01-05
© 2005 by Zeezok Publishing

Published by:
Zeezok Publishing
PO Box 1960
Elyria, OH 44036

www.Zeezok.com
1-800-749-1681

Map of the major cities Haydn visited

Haydn's World and Place in Musical History

Middle Ages	450 – 1450
Renaissance	1450 – 1600
Baroque	1600 – 1750
Classical (Joseph Haydn 1732 – 1809)	**1750 – 1820**
Romantic	1820 – 1900
20th Century or New Music	1900 – Present

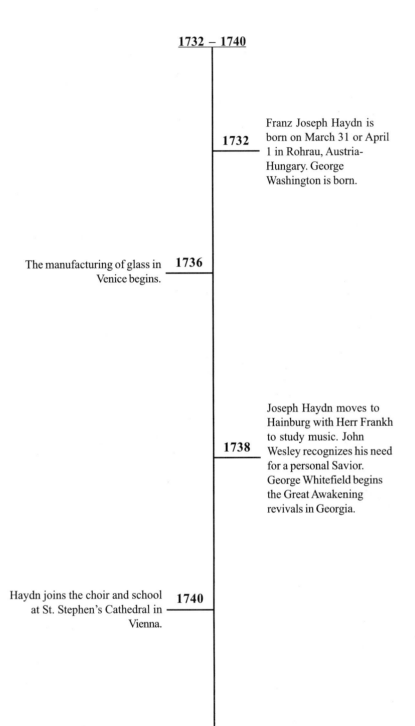

1732 – 1740

1732 Franz Joseph Haydn is born on March 31 or April 1 in Rohrau, Austria-Hungary. George Washington is born.

The manufacturing of glass in Venice begins. **1736**

1738 Joseph Haydn moves to Hainburg with Herr Frankh to study music. John Wesley recognizes his need for a personal Savior. George Whitefield begins the Great Awakening revivals in Georgia.

Haydn joins the choir and school at St. Stephen's Cathedral in Vienna. **1740**

Chapter 1 – A Peasant Boy in Rohrau

Reading Comprehension Questions

1. What did Matthias Haydn (Joseph's father) do for a living?
   • He was a wheelwright, pp. 9, 11.
2. Who came to visit the Haydn family in Rohrau? And what instrument did he bring?
   • Cousin Matthias Frankh from Hainburg who brought his violin with him, p. 11.
3. What did Sepperl (Joseph) use for his make-believe violin?
   • Two smooth pieces of wood, p. 13.
4. What did Cousin Frankh offer to do for the Haydn family — especially for Joseph?
   • He offered to take Joseph to Hainburg to teach him music (the clavier, violin, and singing), p. 13.
5. What did Cousin Frankh teach six-year-old Joseph to play for a big procession in Hainburg?
   • The drum, p. 23.
6. Why did Herr Reutter come from Vienna to Cousin Frankh's house?
   • He was looking for boys to sing in his choir at St. Stephen's Cathedral, p. 24.
7. What was Joseph's reward from Herr Reutter for learning to trill when he sang?
   • He received a plateful of fresh cherries, and he was given the opportunity to become a choir boy at St. Stephen's, pp. 26, 27.

Character Qualities

Humility (pp. 16, 20) – Joseph was reared in a simple thatched roof cottage (p. 16). His father was a hard-working wagonmaker and repairman, not a high-paying job. Joseph learned how to sing masses at Cousin Frankh's church, humbly taking his share of punishments for missed notes (p. 20).

Attentiveness – Joseph listened attentively to many things: Herr Kreutter's market stories at the fruit stall (p. 10), his father's singing (p. 11), the rhythm of the music at the impromptu concerts at home (p. 13), his mother's advice (p. 16), the masses that the older boys sang in church (pp. 19, 20), Herr Frankh's drum training (pp. 22, 23), and Herr Reutter's trilling instructions (p. 25).

Fearlessness (pp. 18, 27) – Although he was only six years old, Joseph was not afraid to leave home (on his parents' counsel and instruction, mind you) for the sake of learning music (p. 18). He later approached the move to Vienna with the same boldness, readying himself with hard work and practice so he could become a Viennese choir boy (p. 27).

Neatness (pp. 16, 20) – Yes, this is an admirable character quality…believe it or not! Perhaps Joseph's *obedience* to his mother's advice to keep clean and neat (p. 16) is as admirable as his attempts to keep clean (p. 20). It's also significant that Joseph had already learned this quality at only six years of age.

Tidbits of Interest

Page 9 – Rohrau is a small village in what is now Eastern Austria near the border of Hungary. The name Rohrau literally means "reedy meadow," and the countryside surrounding it is flat and marshy.[1] The Leitha river [pronounced *lī'tA*] forms the border between Austria and Hungary. It has a tendency to flood the region, making Rohrau a marshy district.

Franz Joseph Haydn was born on March 31 or April 1, 1732. Haydn claimed that his "brother Michael preferred to claim that I was born on 31 March because he did not want people to say I had come into the world as an April fool."[2] Sepperl was a nickname given to young Joseph in Austrian fashion, just as it was the custom to call children by their second names rather than their first.[3]

Pages 11, 13 – Matthias Haydn was a master wheelwright who made wheels for wagons, repaired wagons, and even made wagons. He learned to play the harp while traveling through Germany and Austria as a journeyman wheelwright (after his apprenticeship). He loved Austrian and Croatian folksongs, though he couldn't read music.[4] Johann Matthias Frankh (or Franck) was Matthias's cousin from nearby Hainburg who was the schoolmaster and music director at the local church.

Pages 15, 16 – Mother Haydn, formerly Maria Koller, was reluctant to let her six-year-old leave. However, she and Matthias were strong Roman Catholics, and she harbored hopes that Haydn would become a priest.[5] Maria and Matthias had twelve children, but only six survived infancy: three girls and three boys. Haydn later described his mother as "having always given the most tender care to his welfare."[6] His parents instilled in Joseph and his siblings a love of work, method, and cleanliness.[7]

Page 17 – At Hainburg the mountains slope down steeply to the Danube river. The mountains are covered with dense woods and rocks among which appear the ruins of Hainburg castle from the Middle Ages.

Page 20 – Cousin Frankh was a demanding instructor, and Haydn later admitted, "I shall be grateful to that man as long as I live for keeping me so hard at work."[8] Frankh's wife did not wash or repair young Joseph's clothes to the same standard his mother had upheld. "I could not help perceiving, much to my distress, that I was gradually getting very dirty, and though I thought a good deal of my little person, was not always able to avoid spots of dirt on my clothes, of which I was dreadfully ashamed; in fact I was a regular little urchin."[9]

Pages 21–23 – Haydn learned to play the drum for a procession during the Week of the Cross (May 11–18).[10] The drum he played for the procession is still preserved in the church in Hainburg.[11]

Pages 24–26 – In 1740, Karl Georg Reutter, the newly appointed choir master at St. Stephen's Cathedral in Vienna, came to Hainburg in search of new choristers. When Reutter asked Haydn why he could not "shake" or trill, a contemporary of Haydn records that the young boy replied, "How can you expect me to shake when my cousin [Frankh] does not know how to himself?"[12] Reutter then took Haydn between his knees and showed him how to produce the notes in rapid succession in a "good shake" or trill. Reutter immediately rewarded the lad with a plate of fine cherries when Joseph trilled for him. Haydn said he still thought of those lovely cherries whenever he happened to trill.[13]

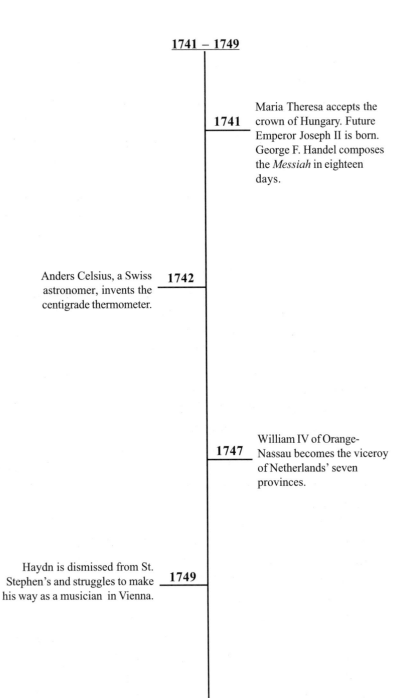

1741 – 1749

1741 Maria Theresa accepts the crown of Hungary. Future Emperor Joseph II is born. George F. Handel composes the *Messiah* in eighteen days.

Anders Celsius, a Swiss astronomer, invents the centigrade thermometer. **1742**

1747 William IV of Orange-Nassau becomes the viceroy of Netherlands' seven provinces.

Haydn is dismissed from St. Stephen's and struggles to make his way as a musician in Vienna. **1749**

Chapter 2 – The Choir of St. Stephen's

Reading Comprehension Questions

1. What were the choir boys' duties in the great St. Stephen's Cathedral?
   • They sang in the processionals at the church services, p. 31. They also sang for special services, feast days, and processionals through the city, p. 33.
2. Why did the boys enjoy singing at the homes of noblemen?
   • They could finally get warm and eat delicious food from the banquet hall, p. 35. Joseph also loved listening to the music, pp. 39, 40.
3. When the choir boys sang at Schönbrunn, the royal palace, what mischief did Haydn become involved in twice? And what was his punishment for such mischief?
   • Joseph climbed the boards and supplies around the new construction on the palace, p. 37. After the Empress had scolded him for doing it, and he dared to do it *again*, Joseph received a caning from Herr Reutter, p. 38.
4. What did Joseph do to improve his musical abilities? (There are several possible answers from this chapter.)
   • He listened to the orchestral instruments playing together at banquets, p. 40. He tried writing his own music in twelve parts, p. 41. Haydn purchased some books on composition and studied them to improve his skills, p. 41. He also worked late into the night trying to rewrite his melodies more beautifully, p. 42.
5. Who else became a choir boy at St. Stephen's and became Joseph's responsibility?
   • Michael, Joseph's younger brother, p. 38.

6. What two things happened that brought an end to Joseph's time at St. Stephen's?
• First, his voice changed and it was not as pleasing to the Empress as it had been when he was younger, p. 44. Second, Joseph was caned and expelled from the choir when he snipped off another choir member's pigtail with his new scissors, p. 45.

Character Qualities

Adventurous (p. 37) – Joseph was ready and willing to explore the palace grounds at Schönbrunn. Moreover, he was at the very top of the boards surrounding the new construction, climbing frighteningly higher and higher.

Creative (pp. 32, 41) – Haydn's creative interests were evident in his willingness to give up play time so he could listen to the organ at the cathedral, and in his efforts to write music in twelve parts though he had little training in composition (p. 41). Joseph's persistence and diligence were also evident in his

purchase of two books on the rules of writing music and in his staying up late to study composition (pp. 41, 42).

Leadership (pp. 38, 39) – Joseph helped care for the younger choir members. Joseph especially worked hard at making life easier for his brother Michael at the cathedral and school. Haydn was also a leader in the gymnastic antics at Schönbrunn, much to the Empress's chagrin.

Mischievousness (pp. 44, 45) – Maybe Haydn's mischievous spirit in snipping the pigtail is not admirable or worthy of imitation, but his fun-loving spirit helped make his music what it became. Joseph's love for laughter, humor, and joyous things affected his compositions, his friendships, and his opportunities in life.

Tidbits of Interest

Page 31 – Vienna was the capital of the Austrian empire during the reign of the royal Hapsburg family (which included Empress Maria Theresa, p. 36). It was also considered the musical capital of the world — filled with thousands of musicians and composers. The splendor of Vienna was at its height in the 1740s, when Haydn was a choir boy at St. Stephen's. St. Stephen's Cathedral has been in the heart of Vienna for centuries. It was built in A.D. 1147, and for many years it was the highest building in Europe, measuring almost 137 meters tall. The Roman Catholic cathedral exemplifies Gothic style, including the gigantic roof, the narrow South Tower, and the tall stained-glass windows.

Pages 32, 33 – Haydn studied music for the church services very carefully, and he claimed that he acquired his practical knowledge of musical techniques by listening to those works. Later in his life, Haydn asserted, "I listened more than I studied. I listened attentively and tried to turn to good account what most impressed me. In this way my knowledge and ability were developed."[14]

Page 34 – Your family will certainly enjoy tasting traditional Austrian cake called *Kugelhopf.*

Kugelhopf

1/2 c. raisins	1 c. sugar
3/4 c. almonds, chopped (optional)	2 tsp. yeast
1-1/2 tsp. grated lemon rind	2 c. milk
6 c. flour, sifted	2 eggs, well beaten
1/4 c. lukewarm water	1/3 c. melted butter
1 tsp. salt	1 tsp. vanilla extract
Confectioners' sugar or icing	

Combine raisins, almonds, and lemon rind with ½ cup flour; toss until well coated. Combine sugar, salt, and 2½ cups flour in large mixing bowl. Sprinkle yeast over water; stir until well mixed. Add yeast mixture to ingredients in large mixing bowl; beat with spoon until smooth. Beat in eggs thoroughly. Add butter gradually beating constantly. Stir in vanilla extract. Add remaining flour; beat until smooth and satiny. Add raisin mixture; mix thoroughly. Cover with towel and let rise in warm place for 1½ hours or until double in bulk. Stir down dough and turn into large, buttered fluted cake pan. Cover with towel and let rise for another hour. Bake in preheated 350-degree oven for about 50 minutes or until cake tester comes out clean. Remove from pan; cool on wire rack. Cover and let stand one day. Sprinkle with confectioners' sugar before slicing, or add thick sugar icing as would Baker Hermann.

Page 36 – Empress Maria Theresa was the Empress of Austria, Queen of Bohemia and Hungary, and wife of Franz I. She ruled the Hapsburg family from 1740–1780. During that time she began many financial, agricultural, and educational reforms that strengthened Austria's economy and resources. Schönbrunn Palace was the Hapsburg showcase for  wealth and architectural greatness, rivaling that of the French royal family at Versailles. Haydn also soon learned that Empress Maria's commands were not to be ignored (p. 38).

Pages 38, 39 – The educational system at St. Stephen's was conducted on a monitorial basis — meaning that the older boys taught the younger ones. Joseph taught his brother Michael. His other younger brother, Johann Evangelist, later became a choir boy at St. Stephen's as well.

Pages 40, 41 – Joseph's musical training at St. Stephen's included singing, violin, and clavier, but not instruction in music theory or composition. Haydn later claimed that he only received two lessons in musical theory from Herr Reutter in his nine years with the choir.[15]

Page 42 – Haydn always found composition to be a labor, but even as a young man he set for himself regular hours to compose.[16]

Pages 45, 46 –With only three ragged shirts, a worn coat, and no money or recommendation, Haydn was dismissed from St. Stephen's at age seventeen on a cold day in November of 1749.[17]

Page 47 – *Andantino* is a moderately fast tempo, faster than *andante*, which is a walking pace.

1750 – 1761

Haydn gets his own attic room and works diligently at composing. Johann S. Bach dies.
1750

1752 Benjamin Franklin invents the lightning conductor. Great Britain adopts the Gregorian calendar.

Maria Antoinette is born. An earthquake in Lisbon kills 30,000 people.
1755

1756 Wolfang Amadeus Mozart is born. The French drive Britain from the Great Lakes in North America.

Haydn becomes a salaried musician at Count von Morzin's home and his first symphony is performed there. The Prince of Esterhazy is in attendance.
1758

1759 G. F. Handel dies. Britain gains Quebec from France. Generals Montcalm and Wolfe are killed in action.

Haydn is appointed as court musician to Prince Paul Esterhazy and then to Prince Nicholas.
1761

Chapter 3 – Wanderings in Vienna

Reading Comprehension Questions
1. When the chapter opened, who helped out young Joseph by giving him food and a place to stay?
   • A singer from another church, Spangler, p. 51.
2. How was Joseph later able to get his own room?
   • A friendly merchant named Bucholz gave Joseph money (150 florins), p. 56.
3. What else did that money allow Joseph to do besides get his own place?
   • He could spend time composing and practicing instead of playing at balls for pay, pp. 52, 56.
4. Joseph began working with music master Porpora. What were some of Joseph's responsibilities?
   • He played the accompaniment for Porpora's singing pupils, p. 61. He also became Porpora's valet: shining his shoes, brushing his clothes, and running his errands, pp. 61, 62.
5. How did Joseph's attitude or nature affect his boss Porpora?
   • His boss was cross and severe, but Joseph's cheerfulness about everything made Porpora more friendly, p. 62.
6. What royal family member requested Joseph to become his Kapellmeister, or music director, at his palace?
   • Prince Esterhazy at Eisenstadt, p. 65.

Character Qualities

Frugality – Joseph worked hard to earn money to survive in Vienna (pp. 52, 59). He rented a cold attic room and used a worm-eaten harpsichord to save money so he could focus on composing and practicing (pp. 56, 57).

Studiousness – Joseph practiced many hours each day to improve his skills and his music (p. 60). He tried to learn as much as possible from music masters he was around. And he listened to the teaching of Porpora (p. 61), the compositions of Gluck and Wagenseil (p. 63), and the ideas of other artists like Kurz (p. 59). His diligence paid off in learning to write quartets and symphonies, and finally being invited to the Prince's palace.

Cheerfulness (pp. 57, 62) – Haydn was happy in spite of his difficult circumstances. He considered himself as fortunate as a king in a palace when he had time to compose, though he was composing in a chilly room with little light (p. 57). Joseph's cheerful disposition even changed his master Porpora's attitude (p. 62).

Tidbits of Interest

Page 51 – Johann Michael Spangler was a singer in another church in Vienna. He and his wife had a nine-month-old son, but they generously invited Haydn to lodge with them in their garret for the winter. Joseph left their home in early 1750 because the Spanglers were expecting a second child soon.[18]

Page 52 – Mariazell [pronounced *mare´ Atsel*] is a village in the province of Styria in east central Europe. It has a 12th-century wood carving of the Virgin and Child that is considered miraculous by many people, and it is visited by thousands of worshipers each year.

Page 55 – The director at the chapel in Mariazell was Florian Wrastil, a former singer at St. Stephen's. Haydn's perfect sight-reading of a difficult solo part earned him the privilege of staying at the chapel for a week. He received good meals for the first time in months, and the singers even took up a small collection for Haydn's return to Vienna.

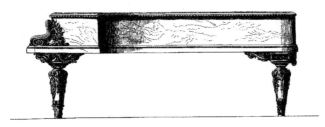

Page 56 – A merchant friend of Joseph's father, Anton Bucholz (or Buchholz, as it is spelled in some documents) lent Joseph 150 florins — interest free and without a date for repayment. Joseph apparently repaid the loan a year after he received it, which was a remarkable feat considering his job situation at the time.[19] In Haydn's will from 1801, he gave to "Fraulein Anna Buchholz, one hundred florins, in as much as in my youth her grandfather lent me one hundred and fifty florins when I greatly needed them…"[20] Haydn rented his own room at the top of a house in Michaelerhaus — a district of Vienna near the Church of St. Michael's (where Spangler sang).

Page 57 – Wheeler and Deucher comment that Joseph "never could be sad about anything for very long." Haydn wanted to make people smile and ease their hardships and troubles.[21] His music was usually joyful and light in style — a style that caused some puritanical church members to criticize his compositions. Haydn's reply was, "Since God has given me a cheerful heart, He will forgive me for serving him cheerfully."[22]

Page 59 – Joseph made extra money by serenading beneath others' windows. Playing beneath Herr Kurz's window was probably no accident. Herr Kurz (or Kurz-Bernardon, as some biographies list him) was a celebrated comedic actor and acrobat in Vienna who had a lovely wife that he would pay musicians to serenade.[23] Herr Kurz was so struck with the originality of Haydn's music that he immediately called on him to write music for a tempest scene in his upcoming opera. This brief musical moment really started Joseph's career as a *composer*.

Pages 60, 61 – Pietro Metastasio lived in the same house as Haydn. He was an Italian poet and librettist who wrote words for operas, oratorios, and so forth. Metastasio brought Haydn a promising young piano pupil who was then ten years old. Marianne Martinez was the daughter of a Spanish nobleman living in the same district of Michaelerhaus, and Joseph taught her for three years in exchange for free food.[24] By the way, Marianne became a leading musician in Vienna — equally talented as a singer, pianist, and composer. She even played duets with Wolfgang Mozart!

Through the Martinez family Haydn was introduced to the famous Italian composer and singing teacher Niccolo Porpora. Porpora gave Haydn valuable criticism on his compositions and helped him improve his Italian.

Page 62 – Haydn apparently helped Porpora improve his temperament. Porpora is described as a man then "sour beyond all that can be imagined,"[25] but Haydn patiently learned by observing Porpora's teaching methods and acting as his valet.

Page 63 – Haydn worked hard to make himself known in Vienna's musical circles. He wrote, "I had to eke out a wretched existence for eight years."[26] To be acknowledged eventually by musicians like Gluck and Wagenseil was a huge achievement. Christoph von Gluck (1714–1787) was a reformer of opera and lived in Vienna when Haydn met him.[27] Georg Wagenseil (1714–1777) was the court composer and music teacher for Empress Maria Theresa and her family from 1739 to his death. Haydn also joined a musical society where he met Karl Joseph von Furnburg who hired him as a violinist at his country home outside Vienna.

Page 65 – In 1758 Haydn obtained a salaried position with some security as a musician at Count Ferdinand Maximilian von Morzin's home. (Furnburg actually recommended Haydn to the Count.) Morzin's summer residence is where Haydn's First Symphony was performed, with Haydn directing the orchestra from his harpsichord. Prince Paul Anton Esterhazy was present at the symphony, and in 1761 the prince offered Joseph a musical position at his palace in Eisenstadt [pronounced *I´zunshtAt*] in eastern Austria.

Page 66 – Wheeler and Deucher make no mention of Haydn's marriage, perhaps because most biographers record it as an unhappy union. Joseph married Maria Anna Keller, the sister of a violinist from St. Stephen's at the same time that Joseph was a choir boy. Maria was three years older than Joseph, and was unable to provide him with children. She seemed indifferent to music, as well. She even lined her pastry tins with his manuscripts, or used his compositions as hair curlers! Nevertheless, Haydn remained faithful to her and supported her for the rest of her life. They lived separate lives with Haydn focusing on his music, and Maria devoting her time to the church.[28]

1762 – 1790

A truce is established between Prussia, Saxony, and the Holy Roman Empire. — **1762**

1764 — London introduces the practice of numbering houses.

Haydn becomes the Kapellmeister (Director of Music) at the Esterhazy court. — **1766**

1767 — Maria Theresa and Joseph II introduce educational reforms in Austria.

Future Emperor Napoleon I is born in Corsica. — **1769**

1770 — The "Boston Massacre" occurs between Boston civilians and British troops. Ludwig van Beethoven is born.

Haydn composes his Symphony No. 45, the *Farewell*. — **1772**

1775 — Paul Revere makes his famous ride from Charleston to Lexington. George Washington is made commander-in-chief of the American forces.

The American Revolution. — **1776 – 1790**

1788 — Haydn composes his *Toy* Symphony.

The French Revolution begins. — **1789**

1772 — Prince Nicholas Esterhazy dies. Benjamin Franklin dies. Haydn is retained as Kapellmeister but is, in effect, a free man. He plans to visit England.

20

Chapter 4 – At the Court of Esterhazy

Reading Comprehension Questions

1. Can you list at least three unique forms of entertainment that the Prince provided for his guests at the palace of Esterhazy?
   • Plays and operettas, including some for a marionette theatre, p. 69; fireworks, p. 72; hunting activities, p. 72; food delicacies, p. 72; and new music from Haydn, p. 73.

2. What did Joseph's orchestra fondly nickname him?
   • Papa Haydn, p. 74.

3. Why were the musicians in the orchestra becoming restless and dissatisfied with life at Esterhazy?
   • They needed a vacation, p. 84. They were kept so busy rehearsing and playing concerts that they had no time to visit families or rest, p. 82.

4. How did Haydn finally convince the Prince to let the musicians go?
   • Haydn wrote a symphony, now known as the *Farewell* Symphony, in which each instrument gradually dropped out and the musician left the stage until the final musician walked off the platform, pp. 84, 85. The Prince got the joke and let the men go home.

5. With what famous young composer did Haydn become dear friends?
   • Wolfgang Mozart, pp. 86, 95.

6. To what country was Haydn invited to direct an orchestra for a man named Salomon?
   • To England, p. 94.

Character Qualities

Hard-working (pp. 72, 73) – Haydn not only directed and performed with the Prince's orchestra far into the night, he also woke at daybreak to begin writing new music for the day. He traveled with the orchestra when they were requested to play for the Empress at Schönbrunn Castle. He received daily music orders from Prince Esterhazy (p. 78), and he and his men rarely were allowed to leave the palace of Esterhazy (p. 79). Haydn even played the organ at a nearby village chapel each Sunday (p. 87).

Fun-loving – Joseph basically composed the *Farewell Symphony* as a joke to help the Prince realize that his men needed a vacation (p. 84). He enjoyed vanilla ice cream, fresh fruit, and pastries (p. 87). Now that's sweet fun! He spotted toy instruments at a country fair and incorporated them into a delightful symphony, the *Toy* Symphony (pp. 92, 93). Haydn was obviously a man who *enjoyed* music and didn't take it extraordinarily seriously all the time.

Generous – Haydn encouraged a young composer named Wolfgang Mozart (pp. 86, 87). Joseph played the organ for a small chapel every Sunday (p. 87). And Haydn gave up time and energy to plan a trip to England in order to share his music with new people (pp. 93, 94).

Tidbits of Interest

Pages 69, 71 – The Austrian Court deliberately strengthened the position of Hungarian nobles in order to keep them loyal to the Austro-Hungarian Empire. In this way they maintained indirect control over the Hungarian people. The key family in Hungary in the eighteenth century was the House of Esterhazy. Prince Paul Anton was a lover of music and could perform on both the violin and the cello, but he died less than a year after Haydn's appointment. The royal successor was Paul Anton's brother, Prince Nicholas, who was given the title "Magnificent" for his love of extravagant entertainments and luxurious surroundings.[29] Prince Nicholas visited Paris and was so impressed by the splendor of Versailles that he decided to build a new palace in a waterlogged forest near Lake Neusiedler. This castle became known as the castle of Esterhazá, and it was built in two years (1764–1765). It included a 400-seat theatre and a marionette theatre built like a grotto or a cave. The Prince's own castle guidebook described the grotto as having "walls and niches…covered with different colored stones, sea shells and snails which strangely reflect the light."[30]

Pages 74, 76 – Haydn's special diamond ring mentioned here was something of a good luck charm that Haydn wore when he composed an important work. In fact, one contemporary biographer of Haydn declared, "that when the master forgot to put on the ring no ideas came to him."[31] Please note, however, that Haydn prayed daily before beginning to compose, which one would consider a much more effective approach to writing quality music than wearing a diamond ring.[32]

Haydn's natural gift for dealing with disputes among his musicians and daily problems in the orchestra earned him their respect, and his fatherly care gained him the nickname or title of *Papa*, a title that remained with him throughout his life.

Pages 78, 79 – Haydn became the Kapellmeister at Esterhazá in 1766. Haydn presented himself at midday before the Prince to receive instructions regarding the music to be played.[33] All compositions of Haydn's were to be exclusively for the Prince's use. Haydn also had to train the singers, maintain his own performance skills, and keep the musical instruments in good condition.

Page 84 – While Esterhazá was intended to be a summer residence, it soon became the Prince's permanent home. Because it was built on a plot that flooded, the climate at Esterhazá was frequently poor. The musicians (including Haydn) were often sick because of the swampy dampness. Moreover, Esterhazá was farther from Vienna than Eisenstadt had been. Most of the musicians' families had to live in Vienna because the housing at Esterhazá was not large enough for their families. In 1772, when the Prince did not make his customary visit to Vienna, and the musicians had been separated from their families for nearly a year, they became restless and asked Haydn to convey their displeasure to the Prince in some musical manner. Thus was born Haydn's Symphony No. 45, nicknamed *Farewell*. The Prince took the hint, and preparations for a trip to Vienna were started the next day!

Page 86 – Mozart and Haydn probably first met in Vienna in 1781. They became very close friends, and some believe Haydn's best symphonies were composed after this friendship developed.[34] There was absolutely no rivalry or envy between the two composers. They each respected the other's works, and Mozart valued Haydn's opinion above that of any other musician — even his father.[35] In 1785 Mozart played six new quartets he had dedicated to Haydn. Haydn told Mozart's father that Wolfgang was the greatest composer he had ever known "either in person or by reputation."[36]

Page 87 – It would only be appropriate to serve a meal of macaroni and cheese with ice cream for dessert while reading this chapter of *Joseph Haydn*. Macaroni and cheese actually became popular right around this time in Haydn's life. Thomas Jefferson returned home from a trip to Paris in 1789 with a macaroni mold, and he served macaroni in the White House in 1802. Macaroni and cheese was even considered fancy enough fare to appear on the tables of Italian and French royalty in 1798! And ice cream has been fashionable dessert since all the way back to the 4th century B.C., though it was perhaps more fruit sorbet than the ice and milk concoctions that King Tang developed in China during the Shang Dynasty (A.D. 618–697). Ice cream recipes were brought back to Europe, and creamed ice was very popular in French and Italian courts by the 1600s.

Page 90 – Empress Maria Theresa visited Esterhazá in September of 1773, and she declared that whenever she wished to hear opera performed well, she would travel to Esterhazá.[37] While this was quite a compliment, she never visited again. She was pleased with Haydn's Symphony No. 48 in C when he named it *Maria Theresa* in her honor. In gratitude, she gave him a gold snuff box filled with ducats, or coins.

Pages 92, 93 – Haydn wrote *Toy* Symphony in 1788 for different toy instruments and strings. It is proof that though Haydn had no children of his own, he had a deep understanding of little ones *and* a delightful sense of fun.

Prince Nicholas died in September of 1790, and his son Anton succeeded him to the Esterhazy title, but Anton had no musical interests. In fact, the new prince disbanded the orchestra and choir (keeping only the military band) and kept Haydn on an annual pension. After serving the Esterhazy family for over twenty-nine years, Haydn finally had time to journey abroad. So when Johann Peter Salomon, a brilliant violinist and concert promoter from England, invited Haydn to give a series of concerts in London, the fifty-eight-year-old composer took the opportunity. Salomon's actual introduction to Haydn is recorded as, "My name is Salomon; I have come from London to fetch you."[38]

Page 95 – When Mozart and Haydn said good-bye before Haydn's trip to England, Mozart sobbed, "We shall never meet again."[39] They never did. Less than a year after Haydn's departure, Mozart died (in December 1791). At first Haydn refused to believe the news of Mozart's death because Haydn himself had been rumored as dead in 1778! Haydn was so deeply affected by Mozart's death that he was often moved to tears at the mere mention of Mozart's name.[40]

1791 – 1809

Haydn visits England and receives honorary Doctorate of Music degree from Oxford University. Mozart dies in poverty in Vienna. — **1791**

1792 — Haydn returns from England to Vienna. Beethoven becomes Haydn's pupil.

Eli Whitney invents the cotton gin. — **1793**

1794 — Prince Anton Esterhazy dies and Prince Nicholas II becomes his successor. Haydn makes a second trip to London and writes his final three symphonies.

Edward Jenner introduces vaccination against smallpox. — **1796**

1797 — Haydn composes his *Emperor* Quartet, which becomes the Austrian national hymn.

The Rosetta Stone is found in Egypt and makes the deciphering of hieroglyphics possible. George Washington dies. — **1799**

1804 — Francis, the grandson of Maria Theresa, assumes the title of Emperor of Austria.

Sir Francis Beaufort designs a scale (from 0 to 12) to indicate wind strength. — **1806**

1807 — Robert Fulton's paddle steamer *Clermont* successfully navigates the Hudson River.

Haydn makes his last public appearance at a special performance of *The Creation* in Vienna. — **1808**

1809 — Napoleon's troops invade Vienna, and Haydn is placed under house arrest. Haydn dies May 31.

Chapter 5 – Joseph Haydn Visits England

Reading Comprehension Questions

1. What was Joseph's emotional response to traveling to England? Was he terrified, excited, uncaring, or what?
   • Haydn considered the trip a great adventure, p. 99.

2. What composer was honored by a special festival at Westminster Abbey? (Haydn considered him the "master of us all.")
   • Georg F. Handel, p. 100.

3. Can you explain why Haydn wrote his *Surprise* Symphony?
   • Haydn wanted to startle the ladies who began to doze during his concerts, p. 103. By starting the music slowly and quietly, and then interrupting it suddenly with a crashing chord, he knew he could make the ladies jump and listen.

4. What other famous composer (though he was a budding composer at this point) did Haydn meet in Bonn, Germany, on his way home to Vienna?
   • Ludwig Beethoven, p. 108.

5. What did Haydn's hometown of Rohrau do to honor him?
   • They placed a monument in his honor in Rohrau, p. 109.

6. What was the English response to Haydn and his music during both of his visits?
   • The English loved him and his music, cheering him loudly at concerts, p. 103. They did not want Haydn to leave and gave him many gifts at his departure, p. 113.

7. What did Haydn do to help Emperor Francis celebrate his royal birthday?
   • Haydn wrote a beautiful hymn that became the national anthem of Austria, pp. 114, 115.

8. Haydn has become known as the "Father of the _____."
   • Symphony, p. 118.

Character Qualities

Adventurous (p. 99) – Haydn considered his trip to England a great adventure, even on storm-tossed seas.

Fun-loving – Again, Haydn's humor and love of fun is evident in his music. He wrote the *Surprise* Symphony to startle napping concertgoers (p. 103). And his music is often light and cheerful, like his Gypsy Rondo (p. 112) and the *Clock* Symphony (p. 106).

Appreciative or Grateful – Haydn was appreciative of the mastery of other composers and musicians, as seen in his response to Handel's music at the London music festival (p. 100). He showed his gratitude for a doctorate of music degree that Oxford University gave him by writing a special *Oxford* Symphony (p. 107). And he was grateful to his parents for the humble home they provided for him and for the sacrifices they made to enable him to pursue music (p. 110).

Loyal – While Haydn received more honor in England than in Austria perhaps, he remained loyal to his prince's requests to return to the Esterhazy home (pp. 108, 113). Moreover, he continued writing music for the Esterhazy family gatherings (p. 114). He even wrote a special hymn for Emperor Francis's birthday (pp. 114, 115).

Tidbits of Interest

Page 99 – The narrowest point across the English Channel is the twenty miles from Calais, France, to Dover, England. Haydn was fifty-eight at the time of this journey. He left Calais on New Year's Day, 1791.

Pages 100, 101 – By January 8, 1791, Haydn was already writing a friend to say, "My arrival caused a great sensation throughout the whole city [London] and I was mentioned in all the newspapers for three successive days…Everyone wants to know me…if I wish, I could dine out every evening…I wish I could fly for a time to Vienna to have some quiet in which to work, for the noise in the street is intolerable." [41] In May of 1791, the Handel

Festival at Westminster Abbey took place with over a thousand singers and players of Handel's music, including the *Messiah*.

Page 107 – In July of 1791, Haydn received an honorary Doctorate of Music degree from Oxford University. His Symphony No. 92 in G is known as the *Oxford* Symphony.

Page 108 – Windsor Castle is an official residence of England's royal family and is the largest occupied castle in the world. It is over 900 years old. Haydn played for the Prince of Wales (future King George IV) numerous times during his months in England. In fact, Haydn was invited to Carlton House, the Prince's residence, twenty-six times and even wrote the Prince's favorite punch recipe in his diary.[42]

Haydn returned to Vienna in mid-summer of 1792. He passed through Bonn, Germany, on his way home, and it was there that he met Ludwig van Beethoven. Haydn agreed to give the young composer lessons in composition. Their differing personalities and ages (Haydn was sixty, Beethoven only twenty-two) made a close friendship nearly impossible. Nevertheless, Beethoven respected Haydn immensely — even paying tribute to the aged composer at Haydn's last public appearance by stepping forward to kiss Haydn's hand.[43]

Pages 109, 110 – When Haydn visited Rohrau at the dedication of a monument erected in his honor, "he knelt down and kissed the threshold of the humble cottage he had shared with his parents for less than six years." [44] Haydn was never ashamed of his humble upbringing, and he often went to church in his shirt-sleeves, just as most peasants did.[45]

Page 111 – During Haydn's second trip to London (1794–1795), he took his servant and copyist, Johann Elssler, with him. It was during this visit that he wrote his final three symphonies: Nos. 102–104. Yes, that means that he wrote over one hundred symphonies in his lifetime. No wonder he is called the Father of the Symphony!

Page 113 – Prince Anton died in 1794, and his successor, Nicholas II, asked Haydn to return to Esterházá to reorganize the orchestra and choir that his militarily and politically minded father had disbanded. Haydn left England in August of 1795 with his compositions, earnings from concerts, and numerous gifts — including a talking parrot that was auctioned off for 1,400 florins after the composer's death.[46]

Page 114 – While he was in England, Haydn was impressed by the playing of the English anthem *God Save the King*. Haydn believed the Viennese and Austrian people needed a morale boost during their struggles against Napoleon and the wars surrounding the French Revolution. He thought adopting a patriotic hymn as a national anthem would help, so in January of 1797 he composed his *Emperor* Quartet for a text called "God Save the Emperor Franz." Haydn's work was adopted at once by the people, and it remained the official Austrian national anthem for over a century. You may recognize it better as the hymn "Glorious Things of Thee Are Spoken" (words by John Newton). Emperor Franz was otherwise known as Emperor Francis, the grandson of Maria Theresa. Ironically, in spite of being defeated by Napoleon's armies, Emperor Francis emerged from the Congress of Vienna in 1815 as one of the most powerful of European monarchs.

Page 115 – By early May of 1809, Napoleon's troops invaded Vienna and the city surrendered to the French. Napoleon ordered a guard outside Haydn's home so that the invalid composer could be as comfortable as possible during their occupation of the city. As an act of defiance against the occupying French forces, Haydn played the new Austrian national anthem on his piano each day.

Page 116 – Haydn's last public appearance was on March 27, 1808, at a special performance of his oratorio *The Creation*. Haydn wrote of this work, "Never before was I so devout as when I composed *The Creation*. I knelt down each day to pray to God to give me strength for my work."[47] He explained that his goal was to inspire worship and adoration of the Creator, and to put the listener "in a frame of mind where he is most susceptible to the kindness and omnipotence of the Creator."[48]

Page 117 – At this final concert, Haydn was seated next to Princess Esterhazy, "who wrapped the old man in her own shawl when she noticed him shivering a little. Many other ladies followed her example, and soon Haydn was covered with the costliest of garments." [49]

Page 118 – When the performance ended and the audience applauded, Haydn lifted his hands to heaven and announced, "Not from me – from there, above, comes everything." [50]

Franz Joseph Haydn was a humble, merry little peasant who once stated, "I offer all my praises to Almighty God, for I owe them to Him alone." [51] In his lifetime, he composed over one hundred symphonies, seventy-six string quartets, oratorios, operas, concerti, masses, and dozens of chamber works. In his final days, Haydn expressed the hope "not wholly to die; but to live on in my music." [52] Though Haydn slipped into a coma and died on May 31, 1809, God answered his prayer to live on through his music. His merry music continues to cheer and refresh the weary world of today.

Endnotes

[1] Karl Geiringer, *Haydn: A Creative Life in Music* (New York: W.W. Norton & Company, Inc., 1946), 21.

[2] Neil Butterworth, *Haydn: His Life and Times* (Neptune City, NJ: Paganiniana Publications, Inc., 1980), 9.

[3] Geiringer, *Haydn: A Creative Life in Music,* 21.

[4] Butterworth, *Haydn: His Life and Times*, 9.

[5] Patrick Kavanaugh, *Spiritual Lives of the Great Composers* (Grand Rapids, MI: Zondervan, 1996), 38.

[6] Geiringer, *Haydn: A Creative Life in Music,* 23.

[7] Jane Stuart Smith and Betty Carlson, *The Gift of Music: Great Composers and Their Influence* (Wheaton, IL: Crossway Books, 1995), 48.

[8] Butterworth, *Haydn: His Life and Times*, 12.

[9] Ibid.

[10] Geiringer, *Haydn: A Creative Life in Music,* 24.

[11] Butterworth, *Haydn: His Life and Times*, 12.

[12] Geiringer, *Haydn: A Creative Life in Music,* 28 (quoting from Giuseppe Carpani's biography of the composer).

[13] Ibid., 28.

[14] Butterworth, *Haydn: His Life and Times*, 15.

[15] Ibid.

[16] Smith and Carlson, *The Gift of Music*, 48.

[17] Geiringer, *Haydn: A Creative Life in Music,* 35.

[18] Butterworth, *Haydn: His Life and Times*, 21.

[19] Geiringer, *Haydn: A Creative Life in Music,* 40.

[20] Ibid.

[21] Smith and Carlson, *The Gift of Music*, 50.

[22] Kavanaugh, *Spiritual Lives of the Great Composers,* 40.

[23] Geiringer, *Haydn: A Creative Life in Music,* 41.

[24] Butterworth, *Haydn: His Life and Times*, 24.

[25] Ibid.

[26] Ibid.

[27] Wallace Brockway and Herbert Weinstock, *Men of Music: Their Lives, Times, and Achievements* (New York: Simon and Schuster, 1950), 85.

[28] Butterworth, *Haydn: His Life and Times*, 27.

[29] Ibid., 33.

[30] Ibid., 39.

[31] Geiringer, *Haydn: A Creative Life in Music,* 79.

[32] Kavanaugh, *Spiritual Lives of the Great Composers,* 39.

[33] Butterworth, *Haydn: His Life and Times*, 32.

[34] Smith and Carlson, *The Gift of Music*, 49.

[35] Butterworth, *Haydn: His Life and Times*, 67.

[36] Leopold Mozart, Personal letter dated February 16, 1785.

[37] Butterworth, *Haydn: His Life and Times*, 54.

[38] Ibid., 79.

[39] Brockway and Weinstock, *Men of Music*, 113.

[40] Butterworth, *Haydn: His Life and Times*, 70.

[41] Ibid., 81.

[42] Brockway and Weinstock, *Men of Music*, 116.

[43] Butterworth, *Haydn: His Life and Times*, 135.

[44] Geiringer, *Haydn: A Creative Life in Music,* 23.

[45] Kavanaugh, *Spiritual Lives of the Great Composers,* 42.

[46] Geiringer, *Haydn: A Creative Life in Music,* 137.

[47] Butterworth, *Haydn: His Life and Times*, 121.

[48] Kavanaugh, *Spiritual Lives of the Great Composers,* 40.

[49] Geiringer, *Haydn: A Creative Life in Music,* 170.

[50] Kavanaugh, *Spiritual Lives of the Great Composers,* 42.

[51] Ibid., 41.

[52] Smith and Carlson, *The Gift of Music*, 50.